In Your
Forties
and Still Cool!

THIS IS A PRION BOOK

First published in Great Britain in 2016 by Prion
An imprint of the Carlton Publishing Group
20 Mortimer Street
London W1T 3JW

A CIP catalogue for this book is available from the British Library.

ISBN 978-1-85375-955-0

Printed in Dubai

10 9 8 7 6 5 4 3 2 1

In Your
Forties
and Still Cool!

Humorous and Inspirational Quotes
for those Aged 40 and Beyond

PRION

Contents

Introduction

Life begins at 40 they say – and they've got a point. John Bishop gave up his day job to become a comedian at 40, Suzanne Collins wrote *The Hunger Games* at 46 and Susan Boyle found fame as a singer at 47. So what are you waiting for?

To help you on your way, here is a fabulous selection of quotes from great minds, original thinkers, renowned wits and loved celebrities. Some are funny and some will make you think, others may inspire you, and one or two might remind you that those emerging grey hairs aren't just there to make you look distinguished.

Turning
Forty

"This is something that is happening to me. This is something that I've got to deal with, alright. I'm sorry if that sounds selfish, but it's me, me, me!"

Eddie on turning 40, Absolutely Fabulous

"When you're 20, 30 seems old. When you're 30, 40 seems old. When you're 40, 39 seems so young."

Galanty Miller

"I would say a magical thing happened when the big 40th birthday came. I felt like a light kind of just went off, and maybe that's because I felt like at 40 I had the right to say and be who I wanted to be, say what I wanted to say, and not accept what I didn't want to accept."

Halle Berry

"Thanks to modern medical advances such as antibiotics, nasal spray and Diet Coke, it has become routine for people in the civilized world to pass the age of 40, sometimes more than once."

Dave Barry

"So you're turning 40? That's no reason to lose your feathers! Look on the bright side: birthdays are good for you. Statistics show that people who have the most live the longest!"

Larry Lorenzoni

"Getting old has its advantages.
I can no longer read the
bathroom scale."

Brad Schreiber

"You receive a new mission at
40, a new lease on life! You have
reached a most auspicious number.
Congratulations! And don't worry
about getting old. There are no
wrinkles or grey hair strong enough
to defy the power of 40!"

Elif Shafak

"Figure out a way to embrace 40,
not run from it. What's great about
40? Forty years' worth of friends,
40 years' worth of life lessons,
40 years of honing skills!"

Jessica Holmes

"I was told that when you hit 40
men stop looking at you. It's true,
until you slip on a mini-skirt."

Mariella Frostrup

"Forty is a fine age, a young, strong, powerful, prime-of-life age, a frisky age, a coming-to-maturity age when all things are possible. But beware it is also an apocalyptic number, a number full of climatic warnings."

Margaret Drabble

"Here comes 40. I'm feeling my age and I've ordered the Ferrari. I'm going to get the whole mid-life crisis package."

Keanu Reeves

"By 39-ish, you've tried it all: cigarettes, hot yoga, prescription sleep aids, at-home hair colour, eyebrow threading, energy bars, acupuncture, sparkling water, tap water, Chinese language lessons, Caribbean cruises with your parents and face masks made of unidentifiable yet somehow still organic vegetable products (I don't care what you say; you will never convince me that's avocado). You know what you like – and what you don't."

Jami Attenberg

"What turning 40 means to me?
I need to take my pants off as soon
as I get home. I didn't used to have
to do that. But now I do."

Tina Fey

"Thirty-nine is worse.
When I was 39, all I could think
about was turning 40."

Aerial Leven

"Every man over 40 is a scoundrel."

George Bernard Shaw

"Once a woman turns 40 she has to start dealing with two things: younger men telling her they are proud of her and older men letting her know they would have sex with her."

Amy Poehler

"A 40-year-old woman is only something to men who have loved her in her youth."

Stendhal

"After 40, what is there to get excited about? Sex, money, booze and dessert – and sex and money are complicated, so we end up drunk and chubby."

Nick Griffin

"I'm turning 40 next year; I don't think I could deal with waking up next to a 25-year-old."

Heidi Klum

"No one becomes 40 without
incredulity and a sense of outrage."

Clifford Bax

"No one is young after 40, but one
can be irresistible at any age."

Coco Chanel

"Turning 40 is like someone
dropping a breeze block on you, but
after that it's just a few pebbles so it
doesn't matter."

Noel Fielding

"The first 40 years of life give
us the text: the next 30 supply
the commentary."

Arthur Schopenhauer

"Women deserve to have
more than 12 years between
the ages of 28 and 40."

James Thurber

As Young as
you Feel

"Youthfulness is about how you live,
not when you were born."

Karl Lagerfeld

"Age does not count. It's what you
know about football that matters."

Brian Clough

"But can one still make resolutions
when one is over 40? I live
according to 20-year-old habits."

André Gide

"You are only young once, but you can stay immature indefinitely."

Ogden Nash

"She may very well pass for 43 – in the dusk, with a light behind her."

W. S. Gilbert

"You are as young as your faith, as old as your doubt; as young as your self-confidence, as old as your fear."

Douglas MacArthur

"Nobody grows old merely by living
a number of years. We grow old
by deserting our ideals. Years may
wrinkle the skin, but to give up
enthusiasm wrinkles the soul."

Samuel Ullman

"You spend a much larger part of
your life being old, not young."

Douglas Coupland

"This wine is 40 years old. It
certainly doesn't show its age."

Cicero

"When I was 49, I posed for *Playboy*. I was very flattered to be asked. I was quite honoured, really, considering that most of the models they feature are in their twenties."

Joan Collins

"Inside some of us is a thin person struggling to get out, but she can usually be sedated by a few pieces of chocolate cake."

Jo Brand

"The secret of genius is to carry the spirit of the child into old age, which means never losing your enthusiasm."

Aldous Huxley

"To my 40-and-over crew!
Don't believe the hype...
We DO get better with age!"

Jada Pinkett Smith

"It is never too late to be what you might have been."

George Eliot

"You can be gorgeous at 30,
charming at 40 and irresistible for
the rest of your life."

Coco Chanel

"Age is strictly a case of mind
over matter. If you don't mind,
it doesn't matter."

Jack Benny

"Age is just a number. If someone can perform at 45, who will stop that fellow from playing top-level cricket?"

Harbhajan Singh

"Age is a number and mine is unlisted."

Anon

"The best way to get a husband to do anything is to suggest that he is too old to do it."

Shirley Maclaine

"When I'm playing 'Rock Band',
I'm like, 'Man, someday, later on
in life when I'm a famous rock
star...' Which gets a little harder to
convince myself of as I reach middle
age, but it still happens a lot."

Tim Schafer

"None are so old as those who have
outlived enthusiasm."

Henry David Thoreau

"Life is truly a ride. We're all strapped in and no one can stop it. When the doctor slaps your behind, he's ripping your ticket and away you go. As you make each passage from youth to adulthood to maturity, sometimes you put your arms up and scream, sometimes you just hang on to that bar in front of you. But the ride is the thing. I think the most you can hope for at the end of life is that your hair's messed, you're out of breath and you didn't throw up."

Jerry Seinfeld

"To keep the heart unwrinkled, to be hopeful, kindly, cheerful, reverent, that is to triumph over old age."

Amos Bronson Alcott

"40 isn't old... if you're a tree."

Anon

"Around mid-life everyone goes maniac a little bit."

Tom Berenger

"Rather than trying to look 20 when you're 40, simply look great at 40 and make the 20-year-olds long to look that good when they're your age."

Anon

"Live it up! You're only middle-aged once!"

Martin Luther King Jr.

"Age is opportunity no less than youth itself."

Henry Wadsworth Longfellow

"You hear a lot of people, they turn 40
and it really bugs them and they get
depressed or whatever. I don't know –
I just don't feel that way. I feel 19 years
old all the time. I could easily say,
God, I feel 70. Or maybe I seem like
I'm 70 or 200 or something to other
people, I don't know. My brain feels 19
all the time. And that's a good spot."

Jack White

"The secret of staying young is to live honestly, eat slowly and lie about your age."

Lucille Ball

"There are days of oldness and then one gets young again."

Katherine Butler Hathaway

"To get back my youth I would do anything in the world, except take exercise, get up early or be respectable."

Oscar Wilde

"Not all men fancy 18-year-olds; many of them fancy 16-year-olds."

Kathy Lette

"The forties – when you are old enough to know better but young enough to keep doing it."

Anon

"We are always the same age inside."

Gertrude Stein

"Adulthood is the ever-shrinking period between childhood and old age. It is the apparent aim of modern industrial societies to reduce this period to a minimum."

Thomas Szasz

"A man is only as old as the woman he feels."

Groucho Marx

"Many a 40-year old man thinks he's as good as he never was."

Anon

"When you're 40, you act like 18 one night and feel 118 the morning after."

Anon

"Avoiding maturity is, for many men, not just a cute hobby, but a life's work – often handsomely rewarded in the infantile popular culture of the West."

Michael Leunig

"See, what you're meant to do when you have a mid-life crisis is buy a fast car, aren't you? Well, I've always had fast cars. It's not that. It's the fear that you're past your best. It's the fear that the stuff you've done in the past is your best work."

Robbie Coltrane

"There is a thing called knowledge of the world, which people do not have until they are middle-aged. It is something which cannot be taught to younger people, because it is not logical and does not obey laws that are constant. It has no rules."

T. H. White

"Age is something that doesn't matter – unless you are a cheese."

Billie Burke

"The lovely thing about being
40 is that you can appreciate
25-year-old men."

Colleen McCullough

"Unmarried women in their forties,
with false teeth and tousled hair,
aren't usually held in the highest
esteem by our society. The feeling
seemed to be that if I could be a
success then anyone could!"

Susan Boyle

"I totally relate to Tom Cruise.
He's not crazy, it's just the litany
of the mid-life crisis."

Bret Easton Ellis

"People who say you are just as old
as you feel are wrong, fortunately."

Russell Baker

"We are young only once. After that
we need some other excuse."

Anon

"You're not 40, you're 18 with
22 years' experience."

Anon

"As I have gotten older, I've
discovered the joys of being lazy."

Julie Bowen

"Boys will be boys and so will a lot
of middle-aged men."

Kin Hubbard

"Middle age went by while I was
mourning for my lost youth."

Mason Cooley

"The key to successful ageing is to
pay as little attention to it
as possible."

Judith Regan

"Setting a good example for your
children takes all the fun out of
middle age."

William Feather

The Ageing
Process

"I know 41 is the new 18, but tell
that to my metabolism."

Marian Keyes

"After 21 time goes so fast…
You become 21, you turn 30,
you're pushing 40 and you
reach 50."

Mark Lowry

"At 40, your idea of weight-lifting
is standing up."

Anon

"I don't like new bands. I don't want to be one of those pathetic old men in their forties who knows exactly what 18-year-olds are into."

Steve Coogan

"Whenever I get down about life going by too quickly, what helps me is a little mantra that I repeat to myself: at least I'm not a fruit fly."

Ray Romano

"If a woman tells you she's 20 and looks 16, she's 12. If she tells you she's 26 and looks 26, she's damn near 40."

Chris Rock

"Middle age is having a choice between two temptations and choosing the one that'll get you home earlier."

Dan Bennett

"In your forties you can do
everything you used to do,
but not until tomorrow."

Anon

"No one says 'cool' anymore.
That's such an old-person thing.
Now we say 'coral', as in 'That
nose job is so coral.'"

Pearl Krabs, SpongeBob SquarePants

"The fact was I didn't want to look
my age, but I didn't want to act
the age I wanted to look either.
I also wanted to grow old enough to
understand that sentence."

Erma Bombeck

"Mid-life is that pivotal moment
when you can finally say that
you basically have all your shit
together and then your body
starts falling apart!"

Tanya Masse

"When you are just muscle, you
end up being gaunt in the face, and
that makes you look older by five or
ten years. I don't think of getting
older as looking better or worse;
it's just different. You change and
that's OK."

Heidi Klum

"You've heard of the three ages
of man – youth, age and 'you are
looking wonderful.'"

Francis Cardinal Spellman

"You know you're turning 40 when light from your birthday cake candles significantly contributes to global warming."

Linda Klemanski

"This whole getting older and being responsible thing is getting in the way of my fun."

Anon

"Enjoy yourself – that's what your twenties are for. Your thirties are to learn the lessons. And your forties are to pay for the drinks!"

Carrie, Sex and the City

"I now realize that the small hills you see on ski slopes are formed around the bodies of 47-year-olds who tried to learn snowboarding."

Dave Barry

"Once you get past a wrinkle or two, a woman over 40 is far sexier than her younger counterpart."

Andy Rooney

"I'm at the age where food has taken the place of sex in my life. In fact, I've just had a mirror put over my kitchen table."

Rodney Dangerfield

"Middle age is when you've
met so many people that every
new person you meet reminds
you of someone else."

Ogden Nash

"Some people, no matter how old
they get, never lose their beauty –
they merely move it from their faces
into their hearts."

Martin Buxbaum

"Why should I fill in a census form?
I spent ages filling it in last time and
I didn't win a thing."

Giles Coren

"You don't stop laughing when you
grow old, you grow old when you
stop laughing."

George Bernard Shaw

"Ageing gracefully is one thing, but
trying to slow it down is another."

Courtney Cox

"You know when you are getting old when the gleam in your eyes is the sun hitting your vari-focals."

Anon

"She said she was approaching 40, and I couldn't help wondering from what direction."

Bob Hope

"Women get psychic as they age. You never have to confess your sins to a woman over 40. They always know."

Frank Kaiser

"After 40 a woman has to choose between losing her figure or her face. My advice is to keep your face and stay sitting down."

Barbara Cartland

"At about 40, the roles started slowing down. I started getting offers to play mothers and grandmothers."

Kathleen Turner

"I don't think people change. I think they definitely mature. But I think the essence of what I am today is the same as when I was five years old. It's just maturity. I've become a healthier, fuller expression of that essence."

Ricky Williams

"If it's true the mind is like a sponge, I wish I could squeeze mine out once in a while and get rid of stuff I don't need any more."

Betty Pfizer

"Middle age is when you choose your cereal for the fibre, not the toy."

Anon

"Nothing makes you feel your age like scrolling down to find your date of birth."

Anon

"The first sign of maturity is the discovery that the volume knob also turns to the left."

Jerry M. Wright

"When you reach 40 you can't
do anything every day."

Henry 'Hank' Aaron

"Tyra Banks: You have no real
family, you're on the wrong side
of 40, you're childless and alone.
Somebody close to you said:
'one more flop, and it's over'.
Tugg Speedman: [pause] Somebody
said they were close to me?"

Tropic Thunder

"In your forties, you grow a little
pot belly, you grow another chin.
The music starts to get too loud
and one of your old girlfriends
from high school becomes a
grandmother."

City Slickers

"Being in my forties I still like
hip-hop, but I like it a certain way,
and I know I'm not the only person
who thinks like that, but I could be
the voice for that."

Heavy D

"Forty is when your body gives your brain a list of things it is not going to do anymore."

Anon

"Just remember, once you're over the hill you begin to pick up speed."

Charles Schulz

"Middle age is the time of life that a man first notices – in his wife."

Richard Armour

"I see nothing funny about baldness. The fact that I, personally, have reached age 42 without any significant hair loss does not mean that I have the right to make insensitive remarks about those of you whose heads are turning into mosquito landing zones."

Dave Barry

"I'm in my forties and I'm constantly surprised by how much my childhood still plays a part in my life."

Sara Sheridan

"Age is that perplexing time of life when we hear two voices calling us, one saying, 'Why not?' and the other, 'Why bother?'"

Sydney J. Harris

"At 40, every time you suck in your gut, your ankles swell."

Anon

"That's one of the things we learn as we grow older – how to forgive. It comes easier at 40 than it did at 20."

L. M. Montgomery

"Your forties – when work becomes
a lot more fun and fun
becomes a lot more work."

Anon

"To me, old age is always 15 years
older than I am."

Bernard Baruch

"You know you're getting old
when the candles cost more
than the cake."

Bob Hope

"You start out happy that you have no hips or boobs. All of a sudden you get them and it feels sloppy. Then just when you start liking them, they start drooping."

Cindy Crawford

"There's no such thing as ageing, but maturing and knowledge, it's beautiful. I call that beauty."

Celine Dion

"Age is like the newest version of
software – it has a bunch of great
new features but you lost all the cool
features the original version had."

Carrie Latet

"At 20 you have many desires which
hide the truth, but beyond 40 there
are only real and fragile truths –
your abilities and your failings."

Gerard Depardieu

"I guess real maturity, which most of us never achieve, is when you realize that you're not the centre of the universe."

Katherine Paterson

"I'm a middle-aged dad, which means I have no social time or life to speak of, and so I connect with my buddies with my Xbox."

Dee Bradley Baker

"Is it a coincidence that the Roman numerals for 40 are XL?"

Anon

"Middle age is when you still believe you'll feel better in the morning."

Bob Hope

"Now I'm lucky if I can find half an hour a week to get funky."

Homer Simpson

"When you're 40 and you go to the doctor's they don't try to fix anything anymore. They just look at you and go 'yeah, that starts to happen.'"

Louis C. K.

"The 'I just woke up' face of your thirties is the 'all day long' face of your forties."

Libby Reid

"At 40, I realize that I was built for comfort, not speed."

Anon

"As I grow in age, I value women who are over 40 most of all... A woman over 40 will never wake you in the middle of the night to ask, 'What are you thinking?' She doesn't care what you think."

Andy Rooney

"The forties – when a narrow waist and a broad mind begin to change places."

Anon

"A few people, and I see no reason why we shouldn't beat them to death with sticks, manage to reach middle age with lean, slender bodies."

Dave Berry

"Guys are idiots, until they're what, 40 years old?"

Wes Borland

"I would feel a lot more middle-aged if I knew more 90-year-olds."

Anon

"I'm officially middle-aged. I don't
need drugs anymore, thank God.
I can get the same effect just by
standing up real fast."

Jonathan Katz

"Maturity is a bitter
disappointment for which no
remedy exists, unless laughter
could be said to remedy anything."

Kurt Vonnegut

"What most persons consider as virtue, after the age of 40 is simply a loss of energy."

Voltaire

"The first half of our lives is ruined by our parents and the second half by our children."

Clarence Darrow

"You know you're old when you're watching *The Karate Kid* and you realize you're more attracted to Mr. Miagi than Ralph Macchio."

Hayley Linfield

"Your body changes in ways they never warned you about. I've got these new eyebrows growing in. Feels like fibre-optic cable… like 'Honey! I got guitar string growing out of my head.'"

Tim Hawkins

"You can only perceive real beauty in a person as they get older."

Anouk Aimée

"Ageing is no fun for men. All we have to look forward to as we drift towards our fifties is wearing leather trousers and hanging round the back of a lap-dancing clubs crying 'But Aurora! This is real!'"

Dara Ó Briain

"Between childhood, boyhood, adolescence and manhood (maturity) there should be sharp lines drawn with tests, deaths, feats, rites, stories, songs and judgments."

Jim Morrison

"I left rock and roll professionally at about 49. That's too long as far as I'm concerned. Some people can do it; it depends on what you were."

Grace Slick

"I'm at an age when my back goes
out more than I do."

Phyllis Diller

"In a man's middle years there
is scarcely a part of the body he
would hesitate to turn over to the
proper authorities."

E.B. White

"Middle age is when your age starts
to show around your middle."

Bob Hope

"Is there something in trade that desiccates and flattens out, that turns men into dried leaves at the age of 40? Certainly there is. It is not due to trade, but to intensity of self-seeking, combined with narrowness of occupation. Business has destroyed the very knowledge in us of all other natural forces except business."

John Jay Chapman

"One of the relaxing things about middle age is the realisation that so many problems aren't worth worrying about, because they will shortly be replaced by others, often more interesting; and that a problem isn't always a problem but a fact."

Peg Bracken

"As I grow older, I pay less attention to what men say. I just watch what they do."

Andrew Carnegie

"A man of 40 today has nothing to worry him but falling hair, inability to button the top button, failing vision, shortness of breath, a tendency of the collar to shut off all breathing, trembling of the kidneys to whatever tune the orchestra is playing, and a general sense of giddiness when the matter of rent is brought up."

Robert Benchley

"At 40, you sing along with the elevator music."

Anon

"Years ago we discovered the exact point, the dead centre of middle age. It occurs when you are too young to take up golf and too old to rush to the net."

Franklin Adams

"I can honestly say I love getting older. Then again, I never put my glasses on before looking in the mirror."

Cherie Lunghi

"I'm 45 now. At my age I love sitting so much… If I'm sitting down and someone tells me I need to get up and go to another room, I need to be told all the information why first."

Louis C. K.

"Men who have reached and passed 45 have a look as if waiting for the secret of the other world, and as if they were perfectly sure of having found out the secret of this."

Golda Meir

"The biggest myth is that as you grow older, you gradually lose your interest in sex. This myth probably got started because younger people seem to want to have sex with each other at every available opportunity, including traffic lights, whereas older people are more likely to reserve their sexual activities for special occasions such as the installation of a new pope."

Dave Barry

"When 40 winters shall besiege
thy brow,
And dig deep trenches in
thy beauty's field,
Thy youth's proud livery so
gazed on now,
Will be a totter'd weed of
small worth held."

Shakespeare, Sonnet II

"No normal man ever fell in love
after 30 when the kidneys begin
to disintegrate."

H. L. Mencken

"You learn when you're in your twenties. You live when you're in your thirties. When you're in your forties, you learn that everything you learned in your twenties was wrong."

Galanty Miller

"Youth looks ahead, old age looks back, middle age looks worried."

Anon

Celebrities
in their
Forties

"Now I'm in my forties I don't feel obligated to do things I don't want to do. I've got to the point where I know my own mind. I'm just more content now. I think that being happy with how you look is sexier than a line-free face."

Melanie Sykes

"When I turned 40, I was like, huh. I accept myself more now. It was much more comforting."

Jennifer Lopez

"I want to enjoy my forties. And yes,
I've got wrinkles, but I'm happy.
I love ageing. I just want to feel
good, I don't want to be scared.
We're all going to get wrinkly
and we're all going to die.
So, just don't resist it."

Natalie Imbruglia

"Happiness is good health
and a bad memory."

Ingrid Bergman

"The financing of all TV shows
is dictated by finding an audience
between 18 and 49. I have now passed
beyond 49, so probably I am no longer
a desirable commodity for TV. And
I am at peace with that; that's fine."

Hugh Laurie

"I played tennis for years, but you
can't improve your game after
you are 50. You get to be 40 and
suddenly you're a doubles player."

Jack Nicholson

"I liked turning 40. Maybe I had a crisis earlier or something. Maybe I had it in my thirties. One thing that sucks though is that your face kind of goes and your body's not quite working the same. But you earned it. You earned that, things falling apart!"

Brad Pitt

"Oh, my knee! Oh, ouch!' I don't feel any of those things!"

Jennifer Aniston

"I've had more fun post-40 than I can remember. From a work point of view, a physical point of view, a psychotherapeutic point of view. When am I supposed to freak out? When am I supposed to feel like, 'I think part of maturity is knowing who you are.'"

Rob Lowe

"I have gratitude. I know myself better. I feel more capable than ever. And as far as the physicality of it, I feel better at 40 than I did at 25."

Cameron Diaz

"The public has always expected me to be a playboy, and a decent chap never lets his public down."

Errol Flynn

"I'm actually happier with my body now... because the body I have now is the body I've worked for. I have a better relationship with it. From a purely aesthetic point of view, my body was better when I was 22, 23. But I didn't enjoy it. I was too busy comparing it to everyone else's."

Cindy Crawford

"I was a buffoon and an idiot
until the age of 40."

Madonna

"I'm standing next to this girl who
is 24 years old and I'm in my forties
and there's no difference. Women
need to see that and feel that. You
can't let the fear of what people
might say or think stop you from
doing what you want to do or else
we would never do anything."

Jennifer Lopez

"You don't think I want to be singing '(I Can't Get No) Satisfaction' when I'm 40, do you? Christ on a bicycle, I'd rather be dead!"

Mick Jagger in 1965

"I heard when you turn 40, things start to go a little less sexual… I heard that's when people don't have sex anymore."

Miley Cyrus

"I've never been willing to lie about my age. Why on earth would I want to tell people I'm 35, which I'm not, and have them say, 'Oh that's nice,' when I could tell them I'm 47, which I am, and have them look at me and go, 'Whoa!' I'm not afraid of ageing. I stopped being afraid of life a long time ago."

Sharon Stone

"I think it's better to feel good than to look good."

Tom Hanks

"Being gay and being a woman has one big thing in common, which is that we both become invisible after the age of 42. Who wants a gay 50-year-old? No one, let me tell you."

Rupert Everett

"I do resent that when you're in the most cool, powerful time of your life, which is your forties, you're put out to pasture. I think women are so much cooler when they're older. So it's a drag that we're not allowed to age."

Rosanna Arquette

"I was in the Chilli Peppers at the time and I asked myself, would I be able to wear a sock on my genitals at the age of 40, and they proved me wrong because I guess they're still doing it."

Cliff Martinez

"I mourn the young girl, but I think that what replaces that is a kind of a liberation, sort of letting go of having to hold on to that."

Michelle Pfeiffer

"You grow. You don't want to stay the same. The thing that was great for you before isn't going to be great for you now. A woman should have many faces through her life, not just one face, not just one hairdo, not just one way. You want to keep rediscovering what's fun for you."

Sharon Stone

"I am essentially a middle-aged woman who likes making up weird snack combinations and galloping."

Miranda Hart

Forty and
Fabulous

"Forty – the new F word: fabulous."

Anon

"Age doesn't protect you from love.
But love, to some extent, protects
you from age."

Jeanne Moreau

"One of the good things about
getting older is that you find you
are more interesting than most
of the people you meet."

Lee Marvin

"I'm in my forties. I don't inject my face with Botox. And I've done more work in the past five years than I've probably done in my whole career. You couldn't pay me enough money to go back to being 20. So many tears; what a nightmare it was. It's much better being older."

Robin Wright

"The prime of life is that fleeting time between green and overripe."

Anon

"Maybe at 87 you slow down a drop, but between 44 and 64, there is no difference."

Jessica Hecht

"People always say that I didn't give up my seat because I was tired, but that isn't true. I was not tired physically, or no more tired than I usually was at the end of a working day. I was not old, although some people have an image of me as being old then. I was 42. No, the only tired I was, was tired of giving in."

Rosa Parks

"And the beauty of a woman,
with passing years only grows!"

Audrey Hepburn

"Few women admit their age.
Few men act theirs."

Anon

"Youth is the time of getting,
middle age of improving, and
old age of spending."

Anne Bradstreet

"I do not think I fully recognized what fun meant until I started having sex in my forties. I thought it was just a fantasy being dangled in front of me, this notion of being in your prime, but it is all blessedly true. It is as if all the machinery has finally clicked into gear. I trust myself more; I know my body better; and I don't feel like I have to justify my sexual proclivities."

Jami Attenberg

"My forties are the best time I have ever gone through."

Elizabeth Taylor

"Probably the happiest period in life most frequently is in middle age, when the eager passions of youth are cooled, and the infirmities of age not yet begun; as we see that the shadows, which are at morning and evening so large, almost entirely disappear at midday."

Thomas Arnold

"I love the game so when I stop loving the game is when I'll decide when I'll stop playing. I'm still in love with it so it won't be yet."

David Beckham at 40

"Forty is... an age at which people have histories and options. At 30, they had perhaps less history. At 50, perhaps fewer options."

Ellen Goodman

"Age is relative. Experience is relative. And I think often intensity is confused with maturity."

Laura Marling

"I've led this empty life for over 40 years and now I can pass that heritage on and ensure that the misery will continue for at least one more generation."

Larry David

"One of the many things nobody ever tells you about middle age is that it's such a nice change from being young."

Dorothy Canfield Fisher

"The young may know the rules, but we know the exceptions."

Anon

"A diamond cannot be polished without friction, nor a man perfected without trials."

Chinese proverb

"Scarlett, when you are 45, perhaps you will know what I'm talking about and then perhaps you, too, will be tired of imitation gentry and shoddy manners and cheap emotions. But I doubt it. I think you'll always be more attracted by glister than by gold."

Margaret Mitchell, Gone with the Wind

"As I'm getting older, I'm enjoying my vices so much more because I feel like I've deserved them."

Brooke Shields

"I keep fit. Every morning, I do a hundred laps of an Olympic-sized swimming pool – in a small motor launch."

Peter Cook

"My life, I realize suddenly, is July. Childhood is June and old age is August, but here it is July, and my life, this year, is July inside of July."

Rick Bass

"The best years of a man's life are after he is 40. A man at 40 has ceased to hunt the moon."

George du Maurier

"Marge: Homer, is this the way you imagined married life?
Homer: Yeah, pretty much, except we drove around in a van solving mysteries."

The Simpsons

"I'm a modern man, a man for the millennium. Digital and smoke-free. A diversified, multi-cultural, post-modern deconstruction that is anatomically and ecologically incorrect. I've been uplinked and downloaded; I've been inputted and outsourced; I know the upside of downsizing; I know the downside of upgrading. I'm a high-tech low-life. A cutting edge, state-of-the-art bi-coastal multi-tasker and I can give you a gigabyte in a nanosecond!"

George Carlin

"Knowledge comes, but wisdom lingers. It may not be difficult to store up in the mind a vast quantity of facts within a comparatively short time, but the ability to form judgments requires the severe discipline of hard work and the tempering heat of experience and maturity."

Calvin Coolidge

"Other people get moody in their forties and fifties – get the male menopause. I missed the whole thing. I was just really happy."

Rik Mayall

"I am 46 and have been for some time past."

Anita Bruckner

"Yes, we praise women over 40 for a multitude of reasons. Unfortunately, it's not reciprocal. For every stunning, smart, well-coiffed, hot woman over 40, there is a bald, paunchy relic in yellow pants making a fool of himself with some 22-year-old waitress. Ladies, I apologize."

Andy Rooney

"A man is not old, but mellow, like good wine."

Stephen Phillips

"Being in your forties – any woman
who isn't there yet, I just have to say
to you: euphoria is coming to you."

Tori Amos

"I miss being the age when
I thought I'd have my sh*t together
by the time I was the age I am now."

Anon

"No matter how long he lives, no man ever becomes as wise as the average woman of 48."

H. L. Mencken

"The great comfort of turning 49 is the realization that you are now too old to die young."

Paul Dickson

"Middle age is when you're sitting at home on a Saturday night and the telephone rings and you hope it isn't for you."

Ogden Nash

"Men in their forties are like the *New York Times* Sunday crossword puzzle: tricky, complicated and you're never really sure you got the right answer."

Carrie, Sex in the City

"Almost all enduring success
comes to people after they are 40.
For seldom does mature judgment
arrive before then."

Henry Ford

"I began to understand my
sensations, to know what
I wanted, at around the age of
40 – but only vaguely."

Camille Pissarro

"Men are most virile and attractive
between the ages of 35 and 55.
Under 35 a man has too much
to learn and I don't have time to
teach him."

Hedy Lamarr

"People in their twenties are
Millennials. People in their thirties
are Generation Y. People in their
forties refuse to be labelled."

Galanty Miller

"You do know, I hope, that no man under the age of 40 can even approach fascinating."

Tasha Alexander

"Forties are good! I'm thinking with my brain now, which is a lot more clear, and women seem to appreciate that. It's a wonderful decade where you're in control of yourself, but the women are still interested."

James Marsters

"Oh, my God, my thirties blew!
Forties are great."

Jennifer Aniston

"The only time you really live fully
is from 30 to 60. The young are
slaves to dreams; the old servants
of regrets. Only the middle-aged
have all their five senses in the
keeping of their wits."

Theodore Roosevelt

"If you're 40 years old and you've never had a failure, you've been deprived."

Gloria Swanson

"At middle age the soul should be opening up like a rose, not closing up like a cabbage."

John Andrew Holmes

"I'm aiming by the time I'm 50
to stop being an adolescent."

Wendy Cope

"A man is never completely alone in
this world. At the worst, he has the
company of a boy, a youth, and by
and by a grown man – the one he
used to be."

Cesare Pavese

"Youth is the gift of nature,
but age is the work of art."

Garson Kanin

"Age is the acceptance of a term
of years. But maturity is the
glory of years."

Martha Graham

Words of Wisdom

"You're never too old to
stop learning."

Ian Botham

"You are never too old to
set another goal or to dream
a new dream."

C. S. Lewis

"At 46 one must be a miser; only
have time for essentials."

Virginia Woolf

"It is unthinkable for a Frenchman
to arrive at middle age without
having syphilis and the Cross of the
Legion of Honor."

André Gide

"Mid-life is the time to let go
of an over-dominant ego and to
contemplate the deeper significance
of human existence."

Carl Jung

"The mid-life crisis is just those
times when you're not so into
the things you were when you
were younger."

Jay Kay

"True terror is to wake up one morning and discover that your high school class is running the country."

Kurt Vonnegut

"It is in the thirties that we want friends. In the forties we know they won't save us any more than love did."

F. Scott Fitzgerald

"Age does not diminish the extreme disappointment of having a scoop of ice cream fall from the cone."

Jim Fiebig

"Maturity includes the recognition that no one is going to see anything in us that we don't see in ourselves. Stop waiting for a producer. Produce yourself."

Marianne Williamson

"It takes 20 years to build a reputation and five minutes to ruin it. If you think about that you'll do things differently."

Warren Buffett

"Don't forget to take life one day at a time, because if you miss a day or two it's called being in a coma."

Tom Zegan

"The best years of a woman's life are the ten years between 39 and 40."

Anon

"If you want to be happy, be."

Henry David Thoreau

"A man sooner or later discovers that he is the master-gardener of his soul, the director of his life."

James Allen

"At the age of 20, we don't care
what the world thinks of us; at 30
we worry about what it is thinking
of us; at 40 we discover that it
wasn't thinking of us at all."

Anon

"It well becomes a man who
is no longer young to forget
that he ever was."

Seigneur de Saint-Évremond

"Of middle age, the best that can be said is that a middle-aged person has likely learned how to have a little fun in spite of his troubles."

Don Marquis

"The other day a man asked me what I thought was the best time of life. 'Why', I answered without a thought, 'now.'"

David Grayson

"We don't understand life any better at 40 than at 20, but we know it and admit it."

Jules Renard

"You don't get smarter as you get older. There's just less stupid stuff you haven't done."

Anon

"Keep true to the dream of thy youth."

Friedrich Von Schiller

"Age is a high price to pay
for maturity."

Tom Stoppard

"From 40 to 50 a man must move
upward, or the natural falling off
in the vigour of life will carry him
rapidly downward."

Oliver Wendell Holmes Jr.

"Forty is a most beautiful age for both men and women. Did you know that in mystic thought 40 symbolizes the ascent from one level to a higher one and spiritual awakening?"

Elif Shafak

"Maturity is the ability to reap without apology and not complain when things don't go well."

Jim Rohn

"A woman past 40 should make up her mind to be young, not her face."

Billie Burke

"Be wise with speed; a fool at 40 is a fool indeed."

Edward Young

"It's tacky to wear diamonds before you're 40 and even that's risky."

Truman Capote, Breakfast at Tiffany's

"One of the things I've discovered, thanks to the Japanese, is that you should enjoy yourself. In the old days, I used to think, 'Oh, never be satisfied, never admit to being happy.' But there's no curse in being happy."

Jane Birkin

"The woman who puts the right amount of candles on her cake is playing with fire."

Anon

"When I became a man I put away childish things, including the fear of childishness and the desire to be very grown up."

C. S. Lewis

"You go through life. You try to be nice to people. You struggle to resist the urge to punch them in the face. And for what?"

Moe, The Simpsons

"Maturity is achieved when a person postpones immediate pleasures for long-term values."

Joshua L. Liebman

"One can't judge until one's 40; before that we're too eager, too hard, too cruel, and in addition much too ignorant."

Henry James

"Anyone who stops learning is old, whether at 20 or 80. Anyone who keeps learning stays young. The greatest thing in life is to keep your mind young."

Henry Ford

"A woman telling her true age is like a buyer confiding his final price to an Armenian rug dealer."

Kathleen Madigan

"I think I was 40 before I realized that almost every writer of fiction or poetry who has ever published a line has been accused by someone of wasting his or her God-given talent. If you write (or paint or dance or sculpt or sing, I suppose), someone will try to make you feel lousy about it, that's all."

Stephen King

"Middle age is not the beginning of decline, but a time to reach for the highest in our selves. Middle age is a pause to re-examine what we have done and what we will do in the future. This is the time to give birth to our power."

Frank Natale

"To think, when one is no longer young, when one is not yet old, that one is no longer young, that one is not yet old, that is perhaps something."

Samuel Beckett

"Being your age is hard enough
without having to act it."

Anon

"Know how to behave at a fine
restaurant, which is a telltale
measure of social maturity."

Marilyn vos Savant

"You shouldn't trust anyone who
listens to Mahler before they're 40."

Clive James

"At middle age the soul should be opening up like a rose, not closing up like a cabbage."

John Andrew Holmes

"When you're 20, you love all your friends. When you're 30, you start to lose touch with friends. When you're 40, you realize who your true friends are."

Galanty Miller

"All my life, I always wanted to be somebody. Now I see that I should have been more specific."

Jane Wagner

"People over 40 can seldom be permanently convinced of anything. At 18 our convictions are hills from which we look; at 45 they are caves in which we hide."

F. Scott Fitzgerald

"In my experience, most 45-year-old women understand that they're no longer 22 and dress brilliantly and stylishly. Their husbands, meanwhile, often look as if they're going to a Primal Scream concert by way of Shoreditch… Yes, younger people look good in casual clothes. But, when it comes to dress, youth is an access-all-areas pass. You have passed that stage and when you dress down you look like David Cameron or Tony Blair.

Also, ask yourself why everyone in *Mad Men* looks so good, despite being in their forties and often out of shape. It's because they wear suits all the time. That, really, is all you need to know."

Alex Proud

"At 20 years of age the will reigns; at 30 the wit; at 40 the judgement."

Benjamin Franklin

"Middle age is when a guy keeps turning off lights for economical rather than romantic reasons."

Eli Cass

"True maturity is only reached when a man realizes he has become a father figure to his girlfriends' boyfriends – and he accepts it."

Larry McMurtry

"Women are most fascinating between the ages of 35 and 40, after they have won a few races and know how to pace themselves. Since few women ever pass 40, maximum fascination can continue indefinitely."

Christian Dior

"Youth condemns; maturity condones."

Amy Lowell

"There is only one success –
to be able to spend your life
in your own way."

Christopher Morley

"If you want to look young and
thin, hang around old fat people."

Jim Eason

"Years, lovers and glasses of wine
should never be counted."

Anon